Welcome to this captivating volume o
Books for Adults: Ancient Egypt Scen
mesmerizing book invites you to step back in time and
immerse yourself in the fascinating world of ancient Egypt.

With intricate designs and stunning scenes, you'll have the
opportunity to bring these remarkable illustrations to life
with your own unique style. Each page features a unique
and intricate design, with plenty of details to color and
personalize to your liking.

You'll find yourself lost in the tranquility of coloring, while
imagining yourself exploring the wonders of ancient Egypt.

Whether you're an experienced artist or just starting out,
this book offers the perfect opportunity to unleash your
creativity and express yourself through color.

So grab your favorite coloring tools and let your imagination
take flight as you add your personal touch to the captivating
world of Ancient Egypt Scenes and Pyramids!

Welcome to this captivating volume of ... This mesmerizing book invites you to step back in time and immerse yourself in the fascinating world of ancient Egypt.

With intricate designs and stunning scenes, you'll have the opportunity to bring these remarkable illustrations to life with your own unique style. Each page features a unique and intricate design, with plenty of details to color and personalize to your liking.

You'll find yourself lost in the tranquility of coloring, while imagining yourself exploring the wonders of ancient Egypt.

Whether you're an experienced artist or just starting out, this book offers the perfect opportunity to unleash your creativity and express yourself through color.

So grab your favorite coloring tools and let your imagination take flight as you add your personal touch to the captivating world of Ancient Egypt Scenes and Pyramids.

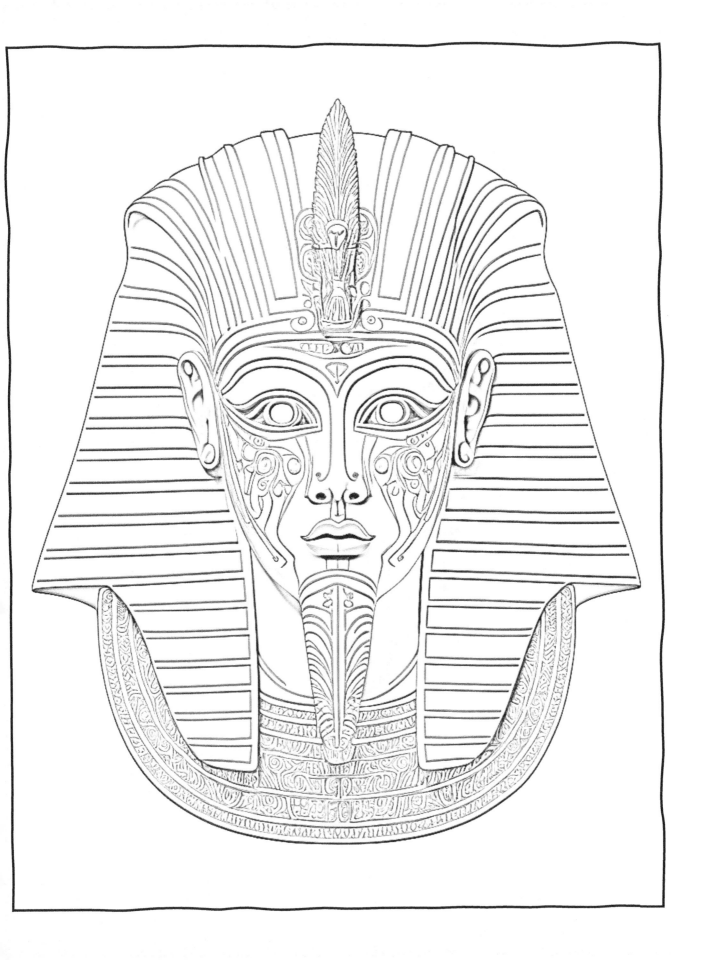

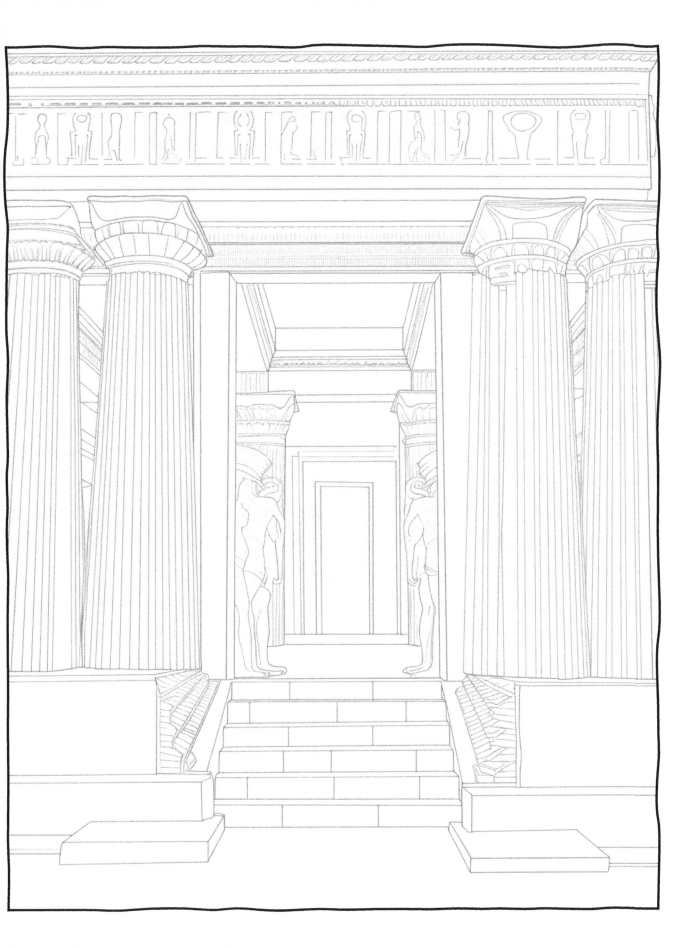

Made in the USA
Monee, IL
04 May 2024

57963656R00057